# RON SANTO

## HEART and SOUL of THE CUBS

**10**

1940–2010

go Tribune Archive Photo

Ron Santo, at home high above Wrigley
Field in the WGN Radio booth.

No part of this publication may be reproduced, stored in a retrieval system, or transmitted in any form by any means, electronic, mechanical, photocopying, or otherwise, without prior written permission of the publisher, Triumph Books, 542 South Dearborn Street, Suite 750, Chicago, Illinois 60605.

Triumph Books and colophon are registered trademarks of Random House, Inc.

This book is available in quantity at special discounts for your group or organization. For further information contact:

**Triumph Books**
542 South Dearborn Street
Suite 750
Chicago, IL  60605
Phone: (312) 939-3330
Fax: (312) 663-3557
www.triumphbooks.com

Printed in the United States of America
ISBN: 978-1-60078-606-8

**Content packaged by Mojo Media, Inc.**
Joe Funk: Editor
Jason Hinman: Creative Director

All photographs courtesy of *Chicago Tribune.*

This book was created by the staff of the *Chicago Tribune* using material from the newspaper's archives.

Alex Garcia

# contents

The life of Ron Santo.................................................7

Chicago Cubs icon
Ron Santo dead at 70.............................................9

Quintessential Santo..............................................21

Cubs lost heart of their organization............29

Remembering Ron Santo.....................................29

Santo gave Chicago his heart...........................41

Santo was nothing fancy.....................................47

Fans tearful at Santo's passing........................55

Tributes to Cubs great Ron Santo..................59

Santo Stats.................................................................68

Santo's numbers Hall Of Fame size................71

Santo: Flag 'my Hall of Fame'...........................81

Best chance at Hall
may come after death............................................89

OUT LOUD with Ron Santo................................93

Santo fights daunting
opponent: diabetes...............................................107

Here's why Wrigley Field
is No. 1 to me...........................................................111

A mensch among boys..........................................115

At home, Santo leaves
the color to the missus.........................................121

# The life of Ron Santo

The longtime Cub's career was marked by excellence in the field and an unflagging love of the team.

## EARLY LIFE/ON THE DIAMOND

**Feb. 25, 1940**
Ronald Edward Santo is born in Seattle.

**1959**
The Cubs sign Santo as an amateur free agent.

**June 26, 1960**
Santo makes his Cubs debut.

**1963**
Makes the first of what will be nine All-Star appearances.

**1964**
Wins the first of five consecutive Gold Gloves.

**1969**
Santo's Cubs, in first place most of the season, go 8-18 down the stretch, losing the division to the eventual World Series champion New York Mets.

**Dec. 11, 1973**
The Cubs trade Santo to the White Sox for Steve Stone, Steve Swisher, Ken Frailing and Jim Kremmel.

**Sept. 29, 1974**
Santo plays his final game, retiring with 342 lifetime home runs, a .277 career batting average and 1,331 runs batted in.

**1979**
The first annual Ron Santo Walk to Cure Diabetes is held as a fundraiser for a disease with which Santo was diagnosed at 18.

**1980**
Santo fails to make baseball's Hall of Fame. It is the first of what will be 19 unsuccessful votes.

## IN THE BROADCAST BOOTH

**1990**
Santo joins the Cubs radio team as an analyst.

**1996**
Announcer Pat Hughes joins Santo in the radio booth.

**Sept. 23, 1998**
In one of his most famous on-air moments, Santo exclaims "Oh no!" after Cubs outfielder Brant Brown drops a fly ball to cost the Cubs a critical late-season game in Milwaukee.

**1999**
Named to the Cubs all-century team.

**2001**
Santo has his right leg amputated below the knee due to complications from diabetes. The following year, his left leg is also removed.

**April 2, 2003**
Santo[1]s toupee catches fire after he gets too close to a space heater in the press box at New York's Shea Stadium.

**Sept. 28, 2003**
Santo's uniform number, 10, is retired by the Cubs.

**2010**
Santo cuts back on traveling with the team due to health concerns.

**Dec. 2, 2010**
Santo dies in Arizona of complications from bladder cancer.

By Paul Sullivan, *Tribune* reporter

# Chicago Cubs icon Ron Santo dead at 70

## Santo never saw Cubs win World Series, never got in Hall of Fame but 'always plowed ahead'

The lasting legacy of Ron Santo — aside from the 342 home runs and five Gold Glove awards, the millions he helped raise for charities and the laughter he provided with his inimitable grunts and groans during Cubs broadcasts — might be the way he lived his life.

"This year" was always the Cubs' year, in Santo's estimation. And when it turned out it wasn't, well, then "next year" would have to suffice.

"Ronnie was a completely unique character," said Pat Hughes, Santo's longtime partner on Cubs radio broadcasts. "There's no way we will ever know someone like him again."

"He always stayed positive, always plowed ahead, and that's why he was loved by Cubs people."

Santo died Thursday night of complications from bladder cancer. Friends of the family said he lapsed into a coma Wednesday at an Arizona hospital. He was 70.

Santo's long-running quests to see the Cubs win a World Series and to be elected to the Hall of Fame never came to fruition. But he firmly believed both dreams would come true, an optimistic outlook that helped him overcome health issues the last 50 years of his life.

What one word best described the Cubs icon?

"Persevere," former Cubs manager Lou Piniella said. "What he went through ... and you never heard a complaint, never heard a bellyache. He always took things in stride, always wanted to see how you were doing. He was a special man, an inspiration to everybody."

After being diagnosed with juvenile diabetes at 18, Santo overcame long odds by not only making it to the majors, but also excelling in a 15-year career. Afterward he survived a bevy of health problems, including cardiac bypass surgery following a heart attack in 1999, the amputation of both legs below the knee in 2001 and '02, bladder cancer surgery in '03 and an irregular heartbeat in '07.

News 720 WGN-AM producer Matt Boltz, who

Ron Santo's infectious smile could be seen all season, even in spring training. Here he is seen in Arizona, signing autographs before a 2003 exhibition game.

worked alongside Santo in the Cubs' booth and became one of his closest friends, said Santo jokingly referred to himself as "The Bionic Man." Despite all the setbacks, he never gave in.

"Ronnie will forever be the heart and soul of Cubs fans," Chairman Tom Ricketts said.

Santo's lifelong love affair with baseball began at an early age. He grew up in Seattle and spent his teenage years working at Sick's Stadium, home of the Seattle Rainiers minor league team. He performed odd jobs every summer, from serving hot dogs in the press box to working on the grounds crew to shining players' shoes.

The Cubs signed Santo after his senior year in high school for $20,000, which was $60,000 lower than an offer he received from the Cincinnati Reds. It wasn't about the money for Santo, who said he wanted to play for the Cubs after falling in love with Wrigley Field watching games on TV.

Ron Santo and then-Cubs manager Dusty Baker (left) share a laugh under the protection of a golf umbrella during a spring training shower. (above) A package of peanuts with an attached note remembering Santo was one of many items placed by fans around the outside of Wrigley Field after news spread of the beloved former-Cub's passing.

On the day following Santo's death, the simple message "#10 Forever" was inscribed on the bill of a Cubs cap and left by a grieving fan on the memorial pavers surrounding Wrigley Field.

Called up from the minors in 1960, Santo went 3-for-7 with five RBIs in a doubleheader at Pittsburgh on his first day as a Cub. He quickly bonded with second baseman Glenn Beckert, and the two would join first baseman Ernie Banks and shortstop Don Kessinger to form the best infield in Cubs history.

Along with his slugging and slick fielding, Santo was known for his fiery demeanor. In manager Leo Durocher's autobiography, *Nice Guys Finish Last,* he addressed Santo's feistiness: "A very emotional kid. He'd get so mad that he'd come in and tear the bench apart. He'd hit the door with his fist. He'd pull the bat rack down, and we'd have to send for the ground crew and have them build us a new one during the game."

That attitude led to a much-publicized incident in 1971 in which Santo choked Durocher during a heated clubhouse meeting. Afterward, Santo went into Durocher's office and persuaded him not to quit. No harm, no foul.

Santo prided himself on playing almost every inning of every game, and he missed only 23 of 1,595 games during a 10-year stretch from 1961 through 1970. He made nine All-Star teams and helped revive a moribund Cubs franchise, but he always will be remembered for the dreamlike 1969 season that ended with a thud.

Losing out to the Mets fed into Santo's long-standing loathing of New York. In 2007, when the Mets were building a new ballpark, Santo told the Tribune he would pay his own way to the Big Apple to "blow up" Shea Stadium.

Ron Santo accepts cheers from the Wrigley faithful on September 28, 2003, in a ceremony to retire his No. 10.

> **Ronnie was a completely unique character. There's no way we will ever know someone like him again. He always stayed positive, always plowed ahead, and that's why he was loved by Cubs people.**
>
> —Pat Hughes, Santo's Cubs radio broadcast partner

"Or maybe even just to watch it blow up," he added with a grin.

After retiring from baseball following a disappointing final season with the White Sox, Santo started a crude-oil company, invested in fast-food franchises, remarried and began the "Ron Santo Walk for the Cure" in 1974, raising tens of millions for the Juvenile Diabetes Research Foundation in the final four decades of his life.

Santo turned down three offers to become an analyst on Cubs radio broadcasts but finally gave in after feeling a buzz while throwing out the first pitch before Game One of the 1989 National League Championship Series at Wrigley Field. Fittingly, Santo's first words on the air on Opening Day of the 1990 season were unprintable. He swore after knocking over a cup of coffee on his scorecard.

When Santo teamed with Hughes in 1996, it turned out to be a match made in Cubs heaven. The combination of Hughes' smooth delivery and dry humor and Santo's blatant homerism and frequent malapropisms was infectious. When Santo screamed, "Oh, no!" after outfielder Brant Brown dropped a fly ball to allow the winning runs to score in a crucial 1998 game in Milwaukee, it was the grunt heard 'round Chicago.

The duo instantly clicked with Cubs fans, forming a lasting relationship that will be difficult to replicate.

"We're both kind of quirky and eccentric," Hughes said. "The mix was unusual and, thankful to say, popular."

Santo's health problems became more of a concern over the last decade. His diabetes caused circulation problems that led to the amputation of his right leg in 2001, then his left leg a year later.

Despite having to learn to walk on two prosthetic legs, Santo rarely missed broadcasting a Cubs game until much later in his career. John McDonough, then the Cubs' vice president of marketing and broadcasting, told Santo, "It's your job as long as you want to do it."

Santo called it his "therapy," despite some terrible Cubs seasons.

In 2003, Santo's son, Jeff, a filmmaker, began making a documentary called "This Old Cub," which centered on Santo overcoming the second amputation, along with his quest to get into the Hall of Fame. When a new Veterans Committee process was introduced in '02, Santo felt like he had a better chance and invited reporters into his Phoenix-area home on selection day.

But the phone call from the hall never came, and Santo fell 15 votes shy of election, beginning a series

Cubs legends (from left to right) Ron Santo, Billy Williams, and Ernie Banks look on during pregame festivities before a cold opening day at Wrigley Field.

Phil Velasquez

of close calls that made the snub more difficult to endure. The Cubs retired uniform No. 10 in his honor in 2003, which eased the pain for Santo, though he admitted he never would "get over" the Hall of Fame snub.

After a roller-coaster 2003 season in which the Cubs came within five outs of their first World Series since 1945, Santo underwent surgery for bladder cancer in late October. He had other health issues over the last seven years but always rebounded.

"Today should be a celebration on the robust life of Ron Santo," McDonough said Friday. "He was really an inspiration to me and to millions of people. ... I think every day for the last 15 years was probably extra innings for him." ∎

*Santo is survived by his wife, Vicki; two sons, Ron Jr. and Jeff; two daughters, Linda Brown and Kelly Reed; and two grandchildren.*

The historic Wrigley Field marquee (left) honors Ron Santo on December 3, 2010, the day after the Cubs legend passed away. Pat Hughes and Ron Santo (above) share a laugh in the dugout before a Cubs home game.

By Paul Sullivan, *Tribune* reporter

# Quintessential Santo

## 10 defining moments

### Heel clicking:

While running to the clubhouse after a thrilling walk-off win at Wrigley Field in June 1969, Santo spontaneously jumped in the air and clicked his heels together a few times. Manager Leo Durocher told Santo to "make that our victory kick," starting a tradition that made Cubs fans roar while infuriating the competition.

### Loathing New York:

Santo's criticism of outfielder Don Young after the rookie dropped a fly ball in Shea Stadium during the heat of the 1969 pennant race was one of several bad memories Santo had of New York. (Years later, Young told writer Rick Talley that Santo was "always the first to speak up for me.") The black cat episode also happened at Shea in '69, the season of the great Cubs collapse. Santo received death threats in New York in 1970 and jokingly requested to "blow up" Shea in '07.

### Headstrong:

Santo was hit in the face with a fastball by Mets pitcher Jack Fisher on June 26, 1966, leading to his left eye being swollen shut, along with a fractured left cheek. No problem. A week later, wearing a specially designed helmet, Santo returned to action and home-red in his first game back.

### Battling Leo:

During a clear-the-air meeting in the Cubs clubhouse in 1971, an enraged Santo began to choke Durocher for claiming the third baseman had demanded that the organization hold a day in his honor. "Maybe I shouldn't have gotten into it with him," Santo wrote in his autobiography. "But my Italian blood was starting to rise." Santo later went to Durocher's office and talked him out of quitting.

Ronnie loved being at the ballpark to talk baseball with anyone who would listen. Whether he was in the club house, on the field or in the dugout, as seen here, he had a story to tell and lessons to teach.

Chicago Tribune Archive Photo

## Gold gloving:

Santo earned five Gold Gloves in his career, earning the reputation as one of the best fielding third baseman of his era. But when the Cubs planned a ceremony in 1966 to present Santo with his '65 Gold Glove, they had to cancel it after the award arrived in three pieces.

## Santo clause:

After the '73 season, the Cubs were breaking up the team and tried to trade Santo to the California Angels. But Santo became the first player to exercise a new clause in the collective bargaining agreement giving veterans with enough years the right to veto any trades. Santo eventually accepted a trade to the White Sox, where he signed a two-year deal before ending his career after one disappointing season.

Ronnie (left) signing yet another autograph for the fans that loved him. (above) Longtime friend and Cubs catcher Randy Hundley greets Santo at home plate after a home run during the 1972 season.

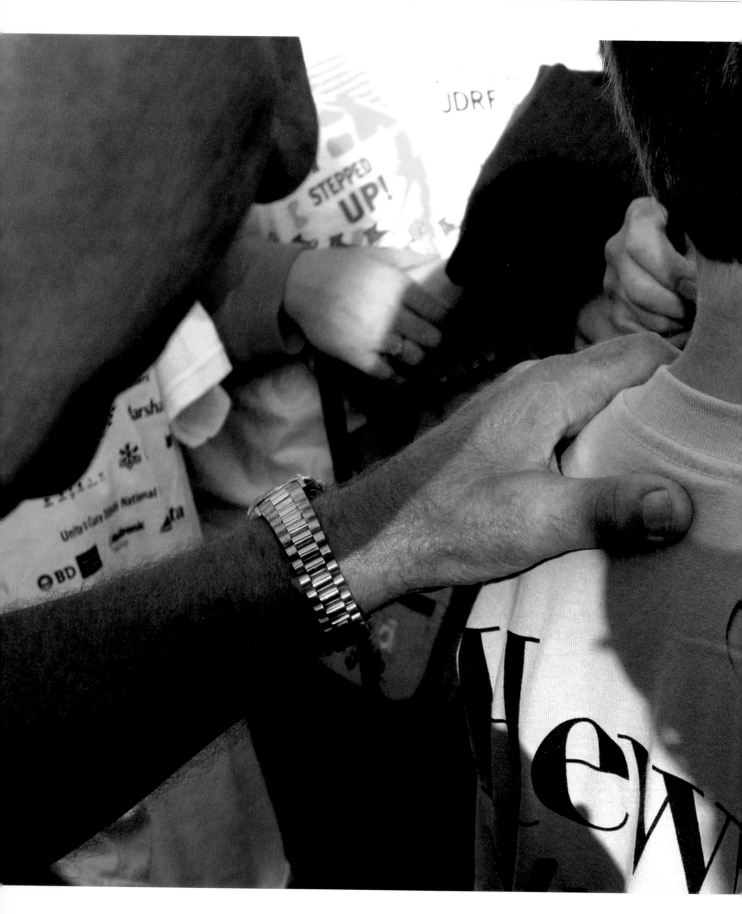

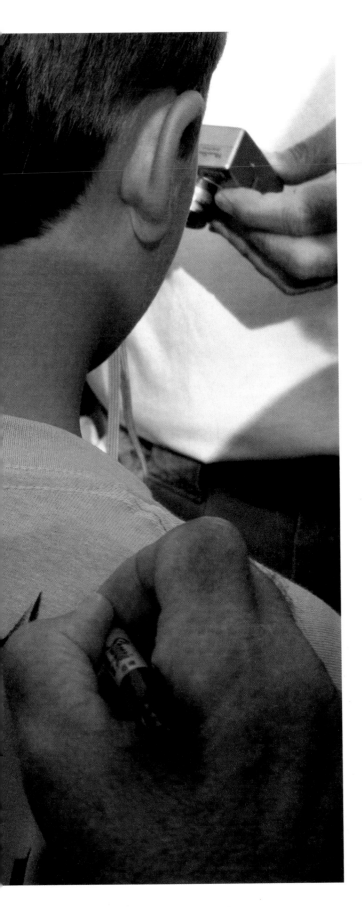

### Walking the walk:

Santo was diagnosed with juvenile diabetes in 1959 but kept it a secret from the Cubs until '63, fearing it would hurt his career. After retiring, Santo raised $40,000 in his first " Ron Santo Walk for the Cure" in Chicago in 1979, and continued to raise millions for the Juvenile Diabetes Research Foundation in the next few decades.

### Oh no!

With the Cubs in a heated wild-card race during the final week of the 1998 season, outfielder Brant Brown dropped a fly ball with the bases loaded and two outs in the ninth inning, allowing three runs to score in a heartbreaking loss to the Brewers at County Stadium. Santo's groan — "Oh no!" — has gone down as one of the most famous phrases in Cubs history.

### Bad hair day:

Santo's toupee was singed while on-the-air during a Cubs-Mets game at Shea Stadium in April 2003. He was standing under an overhead heating lamp when Pat Hughes smelled his toupee burning and threw water on it. At first Santo tried to part his hair with an old comb given to him by Hughes but wound up spiking his hair like a punk rocker.

### Fame game:

While Santo was denied entrance into the Hall of Fame by the Veterans Committee in 2003, the Cubs retired his No. 10 that September in a ceremony at Wrigley Field. "This is my Hall of Fame," an emotional Santo told the crowd. He never made it to Cooperstown while alive. ∎

Another autograph for another fan, but this time it is on the T-shirt of a walker in Ronnie's annual Ron Santo Walk to Cure Diabetes fundraiser in Libertyville, Illinois.

Ron Santo leads members of the Cubs Team of the Century in singing "Take Me Out to the Ballgame" during the seventh-inning stretch at Wrigley.

David Haugh • In the Wake of the News

# Cubs lost heart of their organization

## Who fills that void now?

On the day WGN-AM hired Ron Santo in 1990, he relaxed on a couch in then-general manager Dan Fabian's office as Fabian described a job Santo already relished doing for free.

"Dan said, 'Ron, never stop wearing the blue cap, you are a Cub,' " recalled Chuck Swirsky, WGN's sports director at the time who's now the radio voice of the Bulls. "Ron just looked at him and said, 'You've got it.' "

For the next 20 years, through every "Oh, nooooo!" and oratorical click of the heels, we all got it and everything else Santo had to offer in his own inimitable style.

Santo's unique brand of folksy fanaticism so affected Chicago baseball fans that we will miss it for at least the next 20 years after Santo passed away Thursday due to complications from bladder cancer. He was 70.

This loss will take longer than most for Cubs fans to get over.

"This day and age you get cookie-cutter analysts who are so homogenized that you'll never get another Ronnie," Swirsky said in a phone interview.

The Cubs lost more than a voice in the booth. They lost the heart of an organization, scar tissue and all, who touched the souls of Cub fans across America from ages 8 to 80. A guy who made the confines friendlier every day he came to work at Clark and Addison. The closest thing the Cubs had to a face of the franchise.

Who fills that void now?

You can't replace Santo, you copy his spirit. You find a way to find the good in everything, every day. You laugh at yourself as heartily as you laugh with others. You suffer without complaint and stand tall in the face of disappointment. You battle.

"The biggest fan base lost its biggest fan," said Blackhawks president John McDonough, a member of the Cubs front office for 24 years. "We shouldn't grieve today, we should celebrate a guy who played extra innings for a long time in life. He was a miracle."

A close friend of the family, McDonough recalled a gullibility that humanized Santo in a way that made

Action on the field catches Santo's eye during a game. His cap advertises *This Old Cub*, the documentary about Ron's life produced by his son, Jeff.

"**The biggest fan base lost its biggest fan. We shouldn't grieve today, we should celebrate a guy who played extra innings for a long time in life. He was a miracle.**
—Blackhawks president John McDonough"

him so appealing. On the day in 2003 the Cubs decided to retire his jersey, for example, McDonough called Santo into a roomful of team executives where he began by saying, "We like to get all the right people here, Ronnie, when we deliver bad news ... and his face went ashen."

"That made him easy to tease but you tease the ones you love most," McDonough said.

The Santo you never heard would call terminally ill patients, sometimes during Cubs games, to lift their spirits. The Santo the Juvenile Diabetes Research Foundation came to know raised nearly $60 million over the years with his tireless commitment to the cause.

Words don't do justice describing the way Santo never let suffering from Type 1 diabetes or working as a double-amputee alter his sunny outlook on life. If I tried to tell you the type of daily courage and strength it required, I may start to stammer like Santo trying to get the names right on a 6-4-3 double play.

Smooth, Santo wasn't. That was part of his on-air charm. You didn't listen to the "Pat and Ron Show" (featuring the most patient play-by-play man in the business, Pat Hughes) necessarily for Santo's acu-

men. You listened to hear two guys who genuinely liked each other make baseball sound as much fun as it was when we were kids.

That homespun approach bothered the most uptight baseball fans with little sense of humor or compassion. Santo wasn't for everybody. But the majority of people understood that this was a man who lived to work calling Cubs games more than he worked to live. He didn't need the job. Yet he couldn't fathom living without it.

Even during what will be Santo's last interview on WGN-AM last weekend, he looked forward to another Cubs run at a pennant in 2011 the way he has since first representing the team as a player 50 years ago.

"I think Jim (Hendry) is going to get it done, I really do," Santo said.

He then identified a first baseman, two bullpen arms and a No. 3 starter as Hendry's off-season priorities. He never was more right. Nobody will be more missed.

Harry Caray's legend still dominates Cubs culture after Caray broadcast their games for 15 years. Santo did so for 20.

Near the end, what Santo didn't accomplish annu-

Even though he usually denied it during radio broadcasts, Ron loved getting up in front of the crowd and singing "Take Me Out to the Ball Game" during the seventh-inning stretch. The guest-singer tradition started after the passing of another Cubs broadcasting legend, Harry Caray.

Phil Velasquez

ally overshadowed everything he did. Not being inducted in the baseball Hall of Fame stung.

But every year Santo fell short, I cringed when people expressed pity on his behalf. I never pitied the man. I envied him, and a big reason had nothing to do with winning five Gold Gloves.

Back in 2004, Jeff Santo wrote and directed a documentary called, "This Old Cub," centering around his dad's fight with diabetes. It was a powerful, poignant tribute from a proud son to the father he admired.

Jeff Santo's cinematic labor of love suggested the man who wore the blue cap for millions at work was the same genuine source of warmth and sincerity at home for his kids. There's a shrine for people like that. I can imagine good, ol' No. 10 enjoying it now. ■

Ron Santo discusses things with Yogi Berra (left) during what was almost a historic 1969 season for the Cubs. (above) Santo takes a lap in a golf cart around Wrigley during the ceremony to retire his No. 10.

By Phil Rogers

# Remembering Ron Santo

## Generations of Chicagoans will remember him as the most beloved Cub

Go ahead, Ronnie. Click your heels again. Follow a muttered, "Oh, no!" with stony silence to describe a play that was bungled in true Cub fashion. Tell us what you really think about New York.

Ron Santo is entering a new league, the highest level of all. And there he will never again be betrayed by his passion, his perseverance, his enormous love of life, the joy he found amid more pain and heartache than any dozen men should have to endure.

Bladder cancer reportedly claimed the Cubs' greatest cheerleader, who had battled diabetes for most of his life. He slipped into a coma on Wednesday and died Thursday in Arizona. He was 70, going on 17.

If these things could be measured like runs crossing the plate, the finally tally for Santo would be something like this: Delight 5,410, Bitterness 0.

Well, OK, maybe Bitterness 1.

Santo was never quite sure where to direct his disappointment, but he knew that somebody had screwed him out of his spot in baseball's Hall of Fame, the one he should have reveled in alongside team-mates Ernie Banks, Billy Williams and Fergie Jenkins. It was only natural that slight would trouble him as he celebrated a game that he had loved, even as it changed from small-time enterprise into a $7-billion corporation, complete with phonies and drug cheats, like the two he watched match each other home run for eye-popping home run in the summer of 1998.

From Santo's mouth to your ear, seldom was heard a discouraging word, and that's not a bad measure of the man. No matter the heartbreak, no matter the disappointment, no matter the physical challenge, No. 10 always took comfort in one of the greatest truths about baseball: Tomorrow there's another game.

For generations of Chicagoans, Santo was a reminder that light follows darkness. He wasn't the greatest Cub — that distinction belongs to Banks or Greg Maddux — but he was most assuredly the most beloved Cub, and it would have been wondrous to see him celebrate a championship by the team he joined as a 20-year-old in 1960.

A smiling Ron Santo is shown during happy times in 1969, the near-miss season that would forever haunt him and loyal Cubs fans. Santo did his part for the Cubs in '69, leading the team in home runs (29) and RBIs (123).

> "No matter the heartbreak, no matter the disappointment, no matter the physical challenge, No. 10 always took comfort in one of the greatest truths about baseball: Tomorrow there's another game."

You could almost touch that moment in 2003, but Mark Prior and Kerry Wood couldn't close the deal, and not even Lou Piniella and a $144-million payroll could bring back the magic that died in Game 6. No one was more of a comforter for Prior, Wood and Piniella than Santo, who was installed as the team's captain when Banks and Williams were also in the lineup, and who never really stopped serving. He merely exchanged his bat and glove for a microphone.

In an era before insulin pumps and other innovations of modern medicine, Santo played 15 seasons while battling diabetes, the disease that would eventually claim both his legs before his life. He was scared stiff that it would take him off the field one day, yet he played 2,243 big-league games (all but the last 117 for the Cubs), all the while concealing his illness. He hit .277 with 342 home runs and 1,331 runs batted in. He won five straight Gold Gloves in the 1960s and played in nine All-Star Games.

Bill James, baseball's leading numbers guy, has ranked Santo as the sixth best third baseman of all time, behind only Mike Schmidt, George Brett, Eddie Mathews, Wade Boggs and Home Run Baker. In his book The New Bill James Historical Baseball Abstract, he writes that Santo was a better player than most of the third basemen in the Hall of Fame, even though fewer third basemen have been elected to the Hall than at any other position. He concludes his piece saying that "Ron Santo towers far above the real standard for the real Hall of Fame."

Santo, in my opinion, was excluded for three reasons: His career totals simply weren't gaudy enough; he was placed back onto the Baseball Writers Association of America ballot after being off it for four years, which unintentionally prevented him from ever coming before the old Veterans Committee, and he alienated New York-based BBWAA voters and his fellow players (who would comprise the new Veterans Committee) by clicking his heels after victories at Wrigley Field in the summer of 1969.

Hall of Famer Nolan Ryan recently told me that Santo's heel-clicking rubbed the Mets the wrong way as they reeled in the Cubs. "We didn't think much of that," Ryan said last summer. "In those days, people just didn't do those kind of things."

But Santo wasn't trying to attract attention. He was simply doing what came naturally when overjoyed. The first time he did it, he remembered, was after a Jim Hickman home run capping a four-run, ninth-inning rally against Montreal on June 22, with

Fans didn't realize that 2010 was the last season they'd get to enjoy Ron Santo in the booth and around Wrigley Field. Here he throws out the first pitch during a home game against the Pirates on June 28.

the Cubs on top of the baseball world.

"I was always an emotional player," Santo once said. "I carried my emotions on my sleeve. I ran down the left-field line to our clubhouse and didn't realize I had clicked my heels. That night it was all over television. The next day, when I got to the ballpark, Leo Durocher called [me into his office for] a meeting. He says, 'Can you click your heels again? We ought to make that our victory kick, but only at home when we win.'

"So, from that moment on, when we won at home, I would run down toward our clubhouse doing it. The fans really got into it. I actually got telephone calls from friends on other teams saying, 'Our pitchers don't like that.' My response to them was, 'Too bad.' I ended up getting knocked down a lot, but it didn't matter."

Not a bad epitaph, is it? ∎

Ron (left) always had the pleasure of interviewing "The fine manager of the Chicago Cubs" for WGN Radio pregame broadcast. Dusty Baker's son Darren was trying to be part of the conversation for this interview. (above) Santo rounds third after one of his 17 home runs during the 1972 season.

By John Kass

# Santo gave Chicago his heart

## Cubs legend with passion and with no apologies

My brother Peter, one of two Cubs fans in our baseball-divided family, called to leave a one-word message on a cold morning that was about to get even colder.

"Santo," he said, and I knew.

Many of you most likely received a call just like it, or made one yourself, and said the name just like my brother said it. Santo.

In Chicago, Ron Santo is a name that is all about heart. He wasn't the prettiest baseball player at third base, or the smoothest broadcaster. He wasn't tricky or slick. Sometimes he'd groan in the booth, or cheer, and sophisticated baseball snobs derisively called him a homer because he was such a fan.

Such baseball snobs often treat the game — and all sport — as if it were a bone-dry cathedral built on cold logic, reason and statistics. But if it is a church of sorts, then the fans know it is built on passion and tears.

So, Santo put his heart out there honestly and without reservation every day for decades, on the field and behind that microphone. And by putting his heart out there, he risked it, and Chicago understood and loved him for it.

The calls went out on Friday morning, baseball fans tolling the news that he was gone. Perhaps your heart broke a little, for Chicago and the Cubs and for baseball, and maybe for your own youth, too, if you were lucky enough to see the man play ball.

He'd stand at the plate in the days before batting gloves, stooping to pick up a handful or two of dirt. He'd rub his hands with it, rubbing them past the wrists, to dry them of sweat. Then he'd pick up his bat and stare into the cold eyes of pitchers with names like Gibson, Ryan, Koufax and Drysdale.

Baseball is a game of numbers, and Santo's numbers put him right up there at the top of the game. He was a dangerous hitter in the years of the high pitcher's mound, when dominant pitching was more important to the Lords of Baseball than the pharmaceutically enhanced muscles they embraced years later.

Always with a smile on his face and excitement in his voice, Ron came to the ballpark ready to call the game from his spot in the WGN Radio booth day in and day out.

> **Santo put his heart out there honestly and without reservation every day for decades, on the field and behind that microphone. And by putting his heart out there, he risked it, and Chicago understood and loved him for it.**

The fact that Santo isn't in the Hall of Fame — after a career of five consecutive Gold Gloves, nine All Star appearances and 342 home runs — is an indictment of baseball. Sure, they'll rush to enshrine him now that he has passed away, and further damn themselves for their selfishness.

Yet whatever the Lords of the Game know or don't know, we fans knew. Most of us out in White Sox country on the South Side and in the south suburbs liked him too.

When we were kids — even us Sox fans — we'd go up to the plate at our own fields and pick up the dirt and wash our hands and stare at the pitcher and do a Santo.

"It's that feeling he gave me when he played," my brother said. "Ronnie's uniform was dirty. He'd get the ball and make the play. He did what he had to do."

And that included playing with diabetes and keeping his mouth shut about it until later, when he realized that he could help kids and others suffering from the disease just by talking about it. What was even more impressive is that he did it all without complaint, without seeking any sympathy.

Later, I turned on WGN radio as ace broadcaster Dave Kaplan — another great Cubs fan with one of the biggest Cubs hearts around — was talking about giving Santo a ride home after a Cubs victory.

Santo had gone through that first amputation, and the early prosthetic was causing him problems. There was some bleeding. So, he removed the fake leg and propped it in the car as Kaplan drove.

Dave told him how he'd worn Santo's No. 10 as a Little Leaguer, then looked at the prosthetic and told Santo how sorry he was.

"What are you complaining about?" Santo said. "We won the game, didn't we?"

An entire generation knew Santo from his work in the Cubs broadcast booth on WGN radio as the color man, the analyst, the fan.

But he was a player first, and though he finished his career with the White Sox, he was always a Cub, with 14 years at Wrigley. And he played like he announced.

For those of you who weren't here to understand, back when Santo played in the late 1960s, the city was going to hell. There were riots and protests and more riots and fires. Violence and anger, racial and political, were the lyrics of summer in Chicago.

Ron Santo called Wrigley Field home for 14 of his 15 major league seasons. He loved hitting at Wrigley, racking up 212 home runs, 722 RBI while carrying a .298 average in the Friendly Confines over his career.

Chicago Tribune Archive Photo

Then 1969 happened, and for most of that magical season, the Cubs were in first place and the wild enthusiasm helped heal things. And every game would start with the late Jack Brickhouse's immortal phrase, "Santo, Kessinger, Beckert and Banks, the infield third to first."

After every home victory, Santo would jog toward the clubhouse jumping and kicking his heels for joy.

"I'll never forget how he kicked his heels," Peter said. "The feeling he had when he did it. That feeling he gave us."

And that's how many of us want to remember him, on a baseball field. Jumping for joy, heels clicking like a kid, that great heart pumping. ■

Ron Santo chats with Kerry Wood and fan "Wild" Bill Holden (left) before a game at Wrigley in 2005. Bill had just walked from Arizona to Chicago to raise awareness and money for the Juvenile Diabetes Research Foundation, Ron's favorite charity. (above) Santo, wired for sound, tries to take grounders at third while conversing with his WGN colleagues in 1990.

By Phil Rosenthal

# Santo was nothing fancy

Unpolished, heart-on-his-sleeve ways only deepened the affection of fans and meant everything to Cubs broadcasts

When Cubs radio analyst Ron Santo died Friday at age 70, it triggered a memory of an old "Seinfeld" rerun.

"Maybe I could be like an announcer. Like a color man," George Costanza said. "You know how I always make those interesting comments during the game?"

While humoring his newly unemployed pal by agreeing that he did indeed make good comments, Jerry felt compelled to point out a simple truth.

"Well," he said, as if explaining to a child that people are different from birds, "they generally give those jobs to ex-ballplayers and people that are, you know, in broadcasting."

"Well, that's really not fair," George said, wounded, a response that still gets a smile of recognition from plenty of "Seinfeld" viewers every time it's shown.

Every sports fan thinks he or she could be a color commentator, having offered "interesting comments" to friends, family and other bar patrons for years. But it's like applying for the job of being someone's best friend or favorite uncle or, more precisely, the best friend or favorite uncle of hundreds of thousands of someones.

This is especially true when it comes to the epic, meandering, summer-long conversation that is a baseball season.

Santo was an ex-ballplayer with Hall of Fame-type credentials who didn't dwell on expert analysis, and he rarely came across like a broadcaster even after 20 seasons behind the microphone on WGN-AM 720's Cub-casts.

His popularity and longevity were due to the affection Cubs fans had for him as a player and only deepened as their proxy in the booth and through his playful interaction with play-by-play man Pat Hughes, his broadcast partner the last 15 seasons.

His success illustrates what makes the role of color man so difficult to peg: The best in the business do not share many common threads beyond the fact they wear well and can carry a dull game.

Ron was the Chicago Cubs biggest fan. Being able to bring his excitement and disappointment into the broadcast booth made listening to Cub games on WGN 720 so enjoyable for Cub fans everywhere.

Ron Santo (left) and Billy Williams (right) reminisce about the historic 1969 Cubs season as manager Lou Pinella (center) intently listens to the two Cub legends.

> ## "Santo was an ex-ballplayer with Hall of Fame-type credentials who didn't dwell on expert analysis, and he rarely came across like a broadcaster even after 20 seasons behind the microphone."

Some sagely unlock strategic intricacies, educating the audience and deepening their appreciation of the game. Others seem to be little different than other fans of the home team, only louder. Some push. Some patronize. Some rant and some root. Many are known for patting players on the back, while others are known for spanking them. Some manage to pull off all of that and then some.

And the best broadcast team in baseball is when Vin Scully works alone.

For decades, Scully has been speaking with no one while speaking to everyone on Los Angeles Dodgers broadcasts, weaving a lyrical narrative in which he plays all the parts himself — play by play, expert analyst, historian, humorist, even the sponsors' tout — in monologue form.

Harry Caray had a series of uniformly unremarkable partners on White Sox broadcasts until he was teamed with Jimmy Piersall in 1977. Through 1981, they offered unvarnished, unsparing assessments of what they saw. Sox management came to feel they wanted at least some varnish. But, for fans, the duo was unpredictable, which could not always be said of the teams they covered.

Steve Stone, on White Sox telecasts, adds nuance and insight that makes fans smarter without making it seem as though he's dumbing it down, the way Tim McCarver too often seems to do on national Fox telecasts. On Cubs telecasts, Bob Brenly brings plenty of knowledge, but, just as important, seems to be having a good time with Len Kasper.

Sometimes it boils down to chemistry and comfort. When *Chicago Tribune* parent Tribune Co.'s Cubs and WGN-AM were looking to replace Dave Nelson as a color man on Cubs broadcasts, they hired both Santo and Brenly in 1990, giving Santo a chance to get used to the role in a three-man booth with play-by-play announcer Thom Brennaman.

His successor — Mark Grace, Rick Sutcliffe, Dave Otto, whoever — will not likely get that kind of help. And Hughes' role will change with the new partner. Hughes had to carry much of the burden of telling listeners the what, and often also the why, of what was happening. That left Santo to punctuate what it felt like, for those on the field and in the stands.

When Brant Brown dropped that infamous fly

Santo joined the Cubs mid season in 1960 for his major league debut. For the next 13 seasons he manned the hot corner for the Chicago Cubs, collecting five Gold Gloves and nine All-Star appearances.

ball with the bases loaded and two out in the bottom of the ninth in 1998 at Milwaukee, there were plenty of things that could have been said. Scoff, but Santo' reflexive groan, "Oh, no!" covers it.

Hughes and Santo drew each other out, with Santo sometimes a Gracie Allen to Hughes' George Burns.

Often as not, as the Cubs' chances for a pennant cooled with the weather, they could recast yet another season's dreary diamond drama into something closer to a diverting "Road" picture in the Hope-and-Crosby vein.

The thing about a team that hasn't won a World Series in 103 years and a National League pennant in 65 is its broadcasts can more than occasionally become a show about nothing, and not everyone can successfully pull that off. ∎

Ron Santo was thankful for many things in life. At left, he points at and thanks his family during the ceremony to retire his No. 10. Above, he thanks the Chicago fans at a ceremony in August of 1971.

By Erika Slife, *Tribune* reporter

# Fans tearful at Santo's passing

## Memorial is assembled at Wrigley Field to mark death of legend

The news began to spread at daybreak and, like the winter cold, chilled the hearts of Cubs fans across the city.

Husbands told their wives. A business traveler immediately made plans to visit Wrigley Field. And Cubs staffers held an emotional meeting with the company's president to share a moment of silence – and cry together.

"Ron (Santo) was the voice of the Cubs," said Nicole Jeffrey, of Chicago, who wore a Cubs hat and fought back tears outside Wrigley Field as she paid her respects to the legendary baseball player and lovable broadcaster. "It's going to be a completely different sound."

By mid-morning, mourners had laid Cubs hats and T-shirts, flowers and full cans of beer at the doors and along the sidewalk of the North Side ballpark to honor their beloved icon, who partnered with Pat Hughes on WGN-AM and gave voice to long-suffering Cubs followers everywhere.

"I think it's going to have a huge impact on the fans," said Sherrie Pierce, of Chicago. "Most of the time when I'm watching the Cubs, I'll turn off the TV sound and listen to Ron and Pat."

Those who met him said he was as genuine, friendly and affable as he came across on TV and radio.

"He came in here several times and he was always nice, always polite, a gentleman," said Bradley Rosen, co-owner of CubWorld, a store across from Wrigley Field. An employee unfolded a stack of Santo T-shirts bearing No. 10; orders poured in from all over the country and as far away as Singapore, Rosen said.

"There weren't too many people who didn't love him in the Cubs community," Rosen said.

Peter Chase, director of media relations for the Cubs, said company President Crane Kenney called a staff meeting at 10 a.m. to hold a moment of silence and "share some thoughts and remembrances." Chase described the meeting as "emotional," and said tears were flowing.

Mourners left tokens of appreciation at Wrigley Field on Friday, December 3, 2010, to honor Ron Santo's career as a player and broadcaster for the Chicago Cubs.

Jerry Turner, of Atlanta, was in Chicago for business but stopped by Wrigley Field to take pictures of the scene outside Wrigley, included the famous marquee that read: "Ronald Edward Santo 1940-2010."

"I heard the news and I wanted to come down here," he said. "I just thought he was the greatest Cubs fan ever."

Some fans mourned what they saw as the end of a Cubs era.

"With his passing, and the talk of the expansion of Wrigley Field, it's kind of like the old heritage is being chipped away," said Georgiana Barrie, of Chicago. "I've lived here all my life, I grew up knowing all the older guys – Ernie Banks, Willie Mays, Ron Santo. People didn't trade players all over the place. You were either a Cubs player, or you were not." ■

Fans of all ages gathered on December 3, 2010 at Wrigley field to honor Santo. (left) A flower memorial is left in Ronnie's honor. (above) Mourners look on from the historic corner of Clark and Addison to show their respect.

# Tributes to Cubs great Ron Santo

Ron Santo was a beloved figure and his passing has touched many. Tributes continue to pour in from the sports, broadcasting and even political world. Here's a sampling:

*Cubs Hall of Famer Ernie Banks and Santo's former teammate:*

"It certainly is a sad day for everyone who knows and loves Ron Santo. Ronnie has been a friend of mine for more than 50 years and is like a brother to me. Ronnie's entire life was dedicated to his wonderful family, the Chicago Cubs and their outstanding fans. On the field, Ronnie was one of the greatest competitors I've ever seen. Off the field, he was as generous as anyone you would want to know. His work for diabetes research seemed unparalleled. Ronnie was always there for you, and through his struggles, he was always upbeat, positive and caring. I learned a lot about what it means to be a caring, decent human being from Ron Santo."

*White Sox manager Ozzie Guillen*

"I think it's a very sad day for Chicago and for baseball. You miss a guy who did so much, not just for the Cubs, but for baseball. That's the sad part of this (that he never made it to the Hall). When you talk about Ron Santo, whether you're a Cubs fan, a White Sox fan or a St. Louis Cardinals fan, you're talking about baseball."

*Baseball commissioner Bud Selig:*

"Ron's playing and broadcasting careers shared a common thread: in both capacities, he was a staple of the Cubs' experience every single day. Ron, who overcame so much in his life, was always there for me during challenging times."

Ron Santo puts one over the fence at Wrigley on June 27, 1973.

**Cubs Hall of Famer Billy Williams and Santo's former teammate:**

"Ronnie's passing is a tremendous loss, not only for the Cubs but for all of baseball. He is a man who devoted his entire life to the game, to the Cubs and to the great Cubs fans. He's going to be missed by a lot of people. What I learned from Ronnie is he loved the game, he loved the people in the game and he loved the fans of the game — he enjoyed every moment until the last day of his life. When it came to his beloved Cubs, you never had to look at the scoreboard to know the score of the game — you could simply listen to the tone of his voice. Ronnie was a great friend and will be greatly missed."

**Hall of Famer Fergie Jenkins and Santo's former Cubs teammate:**

"This is a very sad day for Cubs fans and baseball fans everywhere. Ronnie, number 10, was and always will be a Chicago legend. He was a tough player, he wanted to play and contribute every day, and he never let any obstacles stand in his way. Ronnie was one of the leaders on our team. (Manager) Leo Durocher made him the captain, and he took that role very seriously. As an announcer, Ronnie wore his heart on his sleeve. Off the field, his contributions to diabetes research were unmatched. Ronnie will always be remembered as one of the best third basemen the Cubs have ever had, and his number 10 flag flies above Wrigley Field as a tribute to Ronnie."

Ron Santo sits with White Sox owner John Allyn (left) and General Manager Roland Hemond (right) at a press conference to announce him as the newest player on the Chicago White Sox.

**Cubs chairman Tom Ricketts:**
"My siblings and I first knew Ron Santo as fans, listening to him in the broadcast booth. We knew him for his passion, his loyalty, his great personal courage and his tremendous sense of humor. It was our great honor to get to know him personally in our first year as owners. Ronnie will forever be the heart and soul of Cubs fans. Our thoughts and prayers today are with his wife Vicky and their family and we share with fans across the globe in mourning the loss of our team's number one fan and one of the greatest third basemen to ever play the game."

**Chicago Blackhawks and former Cubs president John McDonough:**
"The thoughts and prayers of the entire Chicago Blackhawks organization are with the Santo family. Ron was an inspiration to everyone as his life was defined by overcoming obstacles. It is a sad day for all of Chicago and everyone in the sports world. His incredible passion for the Cubs was unmatched. I was honored to have shared many years of friendship with Ron and will remember those days fondly. Although we collectively are grieving over his passing, we should also celebrate his incredible life."

Hitting the deck once again, Santo dodges a pitch in 1973. Even though the beaning in 1966 shook him up, Santo was never afraid to stand in at the plate against opposing pitchers.

**Cincinnati Reds Hall of Fame broadcaster Marty Brennaman:**
"What a great loss for the Cubs and Cubs fans everywhere. Ron was such a wonderful person and friend. It is so unfortunate that he never became a Hall of Famer, as he should have long ago. It won't be the same for me when the Reds and Cubs play next season and in seasons to come. My condolences to his family and his Cubs family."

**U.S. Representative Mike Quigley of Illinois:**
"This morning, I join Cubs fans across the globe in mourning the loss of one of our own. Ron Santo's joy, devotion, and eternal optimism embodied the best of the Cubs from his All-Star playing days to his years in the broadcast booth. Whether it was clicking his heels at his familiar third base post or leading the fight against juvenile diabetes, Ron wore his heart on his sleeve. He will be missed by everyone who ever had the pleasure to watch him play or hear his voice on the radio, and it is my hope that he will one day take his place among baseball's all-time greats in Cooperstown."

(left) Fans admired Ron for his passion and love of the game, (above) while managers, like Dusty Baker, and players respected him for what he had done on the diamond and the knowledge he could share from his experiences.

### Sen. Dick Durbin of Illinois

"Last night Chicago — and America — lost a hero. Ron Santo was a Chicago Cubs legend and an inspiration to anyone who has ever fought a tough, uphill battle.

"Ron Santo hid his diabetes from the public for ten years because he didn't want anyone to pity him or hold him to a different standard. He wanted to be judged the same way every ballplayer is judged — by the numbers. And by that standard, Ron Santo earned his spot among the greats.

"We can't know how much better Ron Santo's statistics might have been had he not played his entire career with a life-threatening illness, in an era that suppressed the long ball, for a team that, God bless them, never once saw post-season action — but that doesn't matter. Simply put, Ron was the best third basemen in Cubs history and among the best third basemen in the history of the game.

"In September 2003, the Cubs retired Ron Santo's number 10. It now hangs at Wrigley Field, along with the numbers of his former teammates Billy Williams and Ernie Banks. Ron Santo famously said, 'That is my Hall of Fame.'

"But 'This Old Cub' deserved more. Like his fellow Cubs whose retired numbers also hang proudly on the Wrigley Field foul poles — Billy Williams, Ernie Banks, and Ryne Sandberg — Ron Santo should have been in the National Baseball Hall of Fame. That he never made it is the only regret you could have about his career.

"Ron Santo was a ballplayer who lived large, played through unimaginable pain, broadcast the game with all his heart and left an indelible mark on Cubs fans everywhere. Whether he was staring down an opposing pitcher or staring down diabetes, he gave it his all, every day. We will miss him." ■

Ronnie was very open about his disappointment over not being voted by the Veterans Committee into the Hall of Fame, but in 2003 he declared that the retirement of his No. 10 at Wrigley Field was his Hall of Fame.

# Santo Stats

Ronald Edward Santo

**Position:** Third Baseman
**Bats:** Right, **Throws:** Right

**Height:** 6' 0", **Weight:** 190 lb.
**Born:** February 25, 1940 in Seattle, WA
**High School:** Franklin (Seattle, WA)

Signed by the Chicago Cubs as an amateur free agent in 1959. (All Transactions)

**Debut:** June 26, 1960
**Teams (by GP):** Cubs/WhiteSox 1960-1974
**Final Game:** September 29, 1974

## Hitting Stats

| Yr | Team | G | AB | R | H | 2B | 3B | HR | GRSL | RBI | BB | IBB | SO | SH | SF | HBP | GIDP | AVG | OBP | SLG |
|---|---|---|---|---|---|---|---|---|---|---|---|---|---|---|---|---|---|---|---|---|
| 1960 | Cubs | 95 | 347 | 44 | 87 | 24 | 2 | 9 | 1 | 44 | 31 | 5 | 44 | 2 | 2 | 0 | 9 | .251 | .311 | .409 |
| 1961 | Cubs | 154 | 578 | 84 | 164 | 32 | 6 | 23 | 0 | 83 | 73 | 7 | 77 | 1 | 3 | 0 | 25 | .284 | .362 | .479 |
| 1962 | Cubs | 162 | 604 | 44 | 137 | 20 | 4 | 17 | 0 | 83 | 65 | 5 | 94 | 3 | 5 | 2 | 17 | .227 | .302 | .358 |
| 1963 | Cubs | 162 | 630 | 79 | 187 | 29 | 6 | 25 | 1 | 99 | 42 | 7 | 92 | 0 | 11 | 4 | 17 | .297 | .339 | .481 |
| 1964 | Cubs | 161 | 592 | 94 | 185 | 33 | 13 | 30 | 0 | 114 | 86 | 5 | 96 | 0 | 6 | 2 | 11 | .313 | .398 | .564 |
| 1965 | Cubs | 164 | 608 | 88 | 173 | 30 | 4 | 33 | 0 | 101 | 88 | 7 | 109 | 0 | 3 | 5 | 12 | .285 | .378 | .510 |
| 1966 | Cubs | 155 | 561 | 93 | 175 | 21 | 8 | 30 | 0 | 94 | 95 | 7 | 78 | 2 | 8 | 6 | 16 | .312 | .412 | .538 |
| 1967 | Cubs | 161 | 586 | 107 | 176 | 23 | 4 | 31 | 0 | 98 | 96 | 9 | 103 | 0 | 12 | 3 | 17 | .300 | .395 | .512 |
| 1968 | Cubs | 162 | 577 | 86 | 142 | 17 | 3 | 26 | 1 | 98 | 96 | 7 | 106 | 1 | 5 | 3 | 18 | .246 | .354 | .421 |
| 1969 | Cubs | 160 | 575 | 97 | 166 | 18 | 4 | 29 | 0 | 123 | 96 | 7 | 97 | 0 | 14 | 2 | 21 | .289 | .384 | .485 |
| 1970 | Cubs | 154 | 555 | 83 | 148 | 30 | 4 | 26 | 2 | 114 | 92 | 6 | 108 | 1 | 6 | 1 | 17 | .267 | .369 | .476 |
| 1971 | Cubs | 154 | 555 | 77 | 148 | 22 | 1 | 21 | 0 | 88 | 79 | 8 | 95 | 1 | 7 | 0 | 20 | .267 | .354 | .423 |
| 1972 | Cubs | 133 | 464 | 68 | 140 | 25 | 5 | 17 | 0 | 74 | 69 | 5 | 75 | 2 | 8 | 4 | 13 | .302 | .391 | .487 |
| 1973 | Cubs | 149 | 536 | 65 | 143 | 29 | 2 | 20 | 0 | 77 | 63 | 8 | 97 | 0 | 1 | 4 | 27 | .267 | .348 | .440 |
| 1974 | Sox | 117 | 375 | 29 | 83 | 12 | 1 | 5 | 1 | 41 | 37 | 1 | 72 | 0 | 3 | 2 | 16 | .221 | .293 | .299 |
| Career | | G | AB | R | H | 2B | 3B | HR | GRSL | RBI | BB | IBB | SO | SH | SF | HBP | GIDP | AVG | OBP | SLG |
| 15 Years | | 2,243 | 8,143 | 1,138 | 2,254 | 365 | 67 | 342 | 6 | 1,331 | 1,108 | 94 | 1,343 | 13 | 94 | 38 | 256 | .277 | .362 | .464 |

## Fielding Stats

| Team | POS | G | TC | TC/G | CH | PO | A | E | DP | FLD% | RF |
|------|-----|---|----|----|----|----|---|---|----|----|----|
| 1960 Cubs | 3B | 94 | 235 | 2.5 | 222 | 78 | 144 | 13 | 6 | .945 | 0.00 |
| 1961 Cubs | 3B | 153 | 495 | 3.2 | 464 | 157 | 307 | 31 | 41 | .937 | 0.00 |
| 1962 Cubs | 3B | 157 | 516 | 3.3 | 493 | 161 | 332 | 23 | 33 | .955 | 0.00 |
| 1962 Cubs | SS | 8 | 18 | 2.3 | 17 | 6 | 11 | 1 | 2 | .944 | 0.00 |
| 1963 Cubs | 3B | 162 | 536 | 3.3 | 510 | 136 | 374 | 26 | 25 | .951 | 0.00 |
| 1964 Cubs | 3B | 161 | 543 | 3.4 | 523 | 156 | 367 | 20 | 31 | .963 | 0.00 |
| 1965 Cubs | 3B | 164 | 552 | 3.4 | 528 | 155 | 373 | 24 | 27 | .957 | 0.00 |
| 1966 Cubs | 3B | 152 | 566 | 3.7 | 541 | 150 | 391 | 25 | 36 | .956 | 0.00 |
| 1966 Cubs | SS | 8 | 25 | 3.1 | 24 | 7 | 17 | 1 | 5 | .960 | 0.00 |
| 1967 Cubs | 3B | 161 | 606 | 3.8 | 580 | 187 | 393 | 26 | 33 | .957 | 0.00 |
| 1968 Cubs | 3B | 162 | 523 | 3.2 | 508 | 130 | 378 | 15 | 33 | .971 | 0.00 |
| 1969 Cubs | 3B | 160 | 505 | 3.2 | 478 | 144 | 334 | 27 | 23 | .947 | 0.00 |
| 1970 Cubs | 3B | 152 | 490 | 3.2 | 463 | 143 | 320 | 27 | 36 | .945 | 0.00 |
| 1970 Cubs | RF | 1 | 1 | 1.0 | 1 | 1 | 0 | 0 | 0 | 1.000 | 0.00 |
| 1971 Cubs | 3B | 149 | 409 | 2.7 | 392 | 118 | 274 | 17 | 29 | .958 | 0.00 |
| 1971 Cubs | LF | 6 | 12 | 2.0 | 11 | 10 | 1 | 1 | 0 | .917 | 0.00 |
| 1972 Cubs | 2B | 3 | 18 | 6.0 | 17 | 9 | 8 | 1 | 4 | .944 | 0.00 |
| 1972 Cubs | 3B | 129 | 403 | 3.1 | 382 | 108 | 274 | 21 | 19 | .948 | 0.00 |
| 1972 Cubs | LF | 1 | 1 | 1.0 | 1 | 1 | 0 | 0 | 0 | 1.000 | 0.00 |
| 1972 Cubs | SS | 1 | 1 | 1.0 | 1 | 1 | 0 | 0 | 0 | 1.000 | 0.00 |
| 1973 Cubs | 3B | 146 | 398 | 2.7 | 378 | 107 | 271 | 20 | 17 | .950 | 0.00 |
| 1974 Sox | 1B | 3 | 13 | 4.3 | 13 | 13 | 0 | 0 | 3 | 1.000 | 0.00 |
| 1974 Sox | 2B | 39 | 202 | 5.2 | 196 | 97 | 99 | 6 | 40 | .970 | 0.00 |
| 1974 Sox | 3B | 28 | 76 | 2.7 | 74 | 25 | 49 | 2 | 6 | .974 | 0.00 |
| 1974 Sox | SS | 1 | 0 | 0.0 | 0 | 0 | 0 | 0 | 0 | .000 | 0.00 |

### HOME RUNS

| | | |
|---|---|---|
| 1961 | 23 | (15th in NL) |
| 1963 | 25 | (8th in NL) |
| 1964 | 30 | (6th in NL) |
| 1965 | 33 | (4th in NL) |
| 1966 | 30 | (9th in NL) |
| 1967 | 31 | (3rd in NL) |
| 1968 | 26 | (6th in NL) |
| 1969 | 29 | (8th in NL) |
| 1970 | 26 | (19th in NL) |
| 1971 | 21 | (15th in NL) |
| 1972 | 17 | (20th in NL) |
| 1973 | 20 | (25th in NL) |

### RUNS BATTED IN

| | | |
|---|---|---|
| 1961 | 83 | (17th in NL) |
| 1962 | 83 | (18th in NL) |
| 1963 | 99 | (7th in NL) |
| 1964 | 114 | (2nd in NL) |
| 1965 | 101 | (7th in NL) |
| 1966 | 94 | (10th in NL) |
| 1967 | 98 | (7th in NL) |
| 1968 | 98 | (2nd in NL) |
| 1969 | 123 | (2nd in NL) |
| 1970 | 114 | (7th in NL) |
| 1971 | 88 | (12th in NL) |
| 1972 | 74 | (21st in NL) |
| 1973 | 77 | (23rd in NL) |

### AVG

| | | |
|---|---|---|
| 1961 | .284 | (16th in NL) |
| 1963 | .297 | (12th in NL) |
| 1964 | .313 | (7th in NL) |
| 1965 | .285 | (21st in NL) |
| 1966 | .312 | (9th in NL) |
| 1967 | .300 | (12th in NL) |
| 1969 | .289 | (19th in NL) |
| 1972 | .302 | (10th in NL) |

By Jerome Holtzman • *Tribune* reporter

# Santo's numbers Hall Of Fame size

## Going purely by statistics, he should be in

Billy Pierce won 211 games, more victories than 15 of the pitchers in the Hall of Fame, but never received more than 2 percent of the vote and was dropped from the ballot. Luke Appling, a two-time batting champion, among the greatest players in White Sox history, got in through the side door; a special runoff was held because no players were elected in the original voting.

Billy Williams waited six years. Nellie Fox, up there in Valhalla, is still waiting. In 1985, he received 74.68 percent of the vote. It should have been rounded out to the required 75 percent, but the directors of the Hall of Fame, in a burst of stupidity concealed beneath the umbrella of purity, locked Little Nell out, claiming he missed by 32-hundredths of a percent.

Hack Wilson of the Cubs still holds the major-league record for the most runs batted in in one season, 190, but the pearly gates didn`t open until 45 years after he had retired as a player.

When he became eligible in 1979, Luis Aparicio, possibly the best shortstop of the 20th Century, almost didn't make the ballot. Some members of the screening committee scratched him, deemed him not worthy of consideration. Two years later Aparicio received only 12 percent of the vote, barely enough to maintain his eligibility.

The list of the 1989 candidates was announced Wednesday in New York and it occurred to me anew that for the last quarter of a century, with the exception of Ernie Banks (elected in 1977), Chicago players have had to struggle for Hall of Fame recognition. Cooperstown has been cruel to them.

Of the new eligibles, three are likely to be anointed in their first time at-bat: Johnny Bench of Cincinnati, the reigning catcher of his time; Carl Yastrzemski, superstar outfielder with the Boston Red Sox; and pitcher Gaylord Perry, a 300-game winner. Ferguson Jenkins of the Cubs, a seven-time 20-game winner, also is eligible for the first time and worthy of immediate canonization.

Ordinarily I don't pump for Chicago players. It

A lot of Ronnie's milestones as a player are known but here are a few that are rarely mentioned. He led the National League in walks four times (1964, 1966-68), led in triples with 13 in 1964 and won the Lou Gehrig Memorial Award in 1973.

Santo wasn't only popular among fans and fellow baseball players. Here he is seen with the Blackhawks' Reg Fleming before a game in 1963. Ronnie seems amused by Fleming's demonstration of how he would play hockey with baseball equipment.

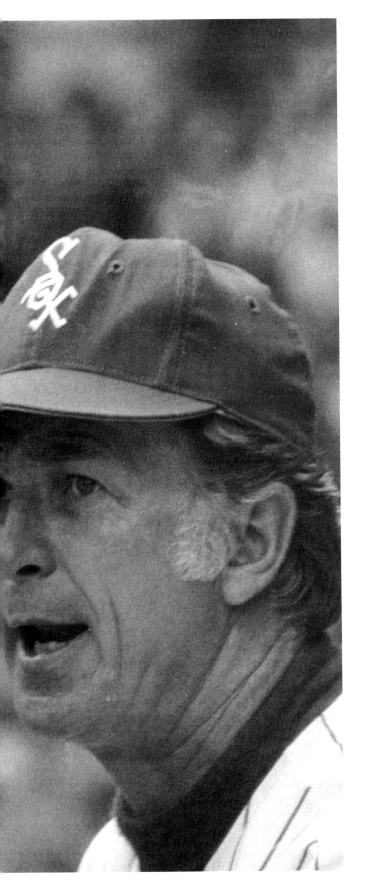

doesn't seem proper. I have preferred to assume it should not be necessary to bang the drum, that the 400-plus voters (10-year members of the Baseball Writers Association of America) constitute an educated and capable electorate.

Then I think of Ron Santo and realize some campaigning is necessary.

A hero Cub in the '60s and '70s, Santo was the best all-around third baseman of his time. Baltimore's Brooks Robinson was, of course, the best fielding third baseman, but Santo was a much stronger hitter. And he was almost B. Robby's equal in the field.

Santo, nonetheless, was virtually ignored in 1980, his first year on the ballot. It is scandalous to recall that he received only 15 of the 385 votes cast, 4 percent. According to the rules, players with less than 5 percent are automatically dropped from the

Santo (left) spent the last season of his career on the South Side of Chicago as a member of the White Sox, his only season not a member of the Cubs. (above) In contrast, Ronnie is seen here just after his rookie season with pitcher Don Cardwell. Both are shown with their awards from the 21st annual Diamond Dinner of the Chicago baseball writers.

Chicago Tribune Archive Photo

ballot. From 1981 to '84, Santo was a nonperson, not welcome in Cooperstown.

The death of Ken Boyer, a star third baseman with the Cardinals, triggered a re-examination of the system. Boyer, too, had been a victim of the 5-percent rule. Bob Broeg, a St. Louis baseball writer, led a movement to reinstate Boyer, insisting Boyer was entitled to another chance.

Boyer's name was restored but with the provision that other worthies, who also had been thrown on the discard pile, would simultaneously be reinstated. Santo was among the players in this group, risen from Boyer's grave. But Santo was to suffer another indignity. The secretary of the BBWAA apparently had forgotten Santo's first name and listed him as Roy, not Ron. Santo drew 13 percent of the vote in '85. His percentage has been increasing steadily. He was on 108 of the 427 ballots in the last election, 25 percent.

Probably because he was such a strong hitter,

Santo never wanted to be in the way of another ball to the head after being hit in 1966. You can see him hitting the deck (left) to avoid a pitch in 1970. (above) Ron greets fans as he enters Wrigley for the 1976 home opener.

Santo, who for many years was the Cub captain, never received much acclaim for his defensive ability. Through hard work and nothing else (he was originally a catcher), he made himself an acceptable third baseman and soon thereafter was the best defensive third baseman in the National League.

As most fans realize, fielding averages are deceptive. The lumbering galoot who can't move off a silver dollar (once it was a dime, but adjustments must be made for inflation) has an enormous statistical advantage. Errors are not charged for slow fielding; the leadfoot escapes because he doesn't reach the ball. The best index of a defensive player's effectiveness is not fewest errors, but chances accepted.

Brooks Robinson, who played eight more years than Santo, is the all-time career leader in chances with 9,165, including errors. But a closer examination reveals that Santo, who had a 15-year major-league career, was the busier third baseman. Santo averaged 457 chances a season compared to B. Robby's 399. Santo averaged more assists, 305 to 270, and more putouts, 130 to 117.

And Santo, of course, was the much stronger hitter with a career total of 342 home runs and 1,331 runs batted in, an average of almost 90 RBIs a season. His power stats (slugging average, home runs and RBIs) compare with those of Billy Williams and Banks, his Cub teammates whose plaques hang in Cooperstown.

"If I'm in, Ronnie should be in, too," Billy Williams said the summer before last, a few moments after he was enshrined.

My sentiments, exactly. ■

Cubs owner P.K. Wrigley (tossing ball) is surrounded by a group of talented young players. From left to right is catcher Dick Bertell, outfielder Lou Brock and third baseman Ron Santo. Bertell and Santo both debuted as Cubs in 1960 and all three players were on the North Side by the end of the 1961 season.

By Bill Jauss • *Tribune* reporter

# Santo: Flag 'my Hall of Fame'

## Ceremony full of emotion as number retired

Two days before Sunday's emotional ceremony at Wrigley Field, a couple of friends asked Ron Santo what it would mean to have the Cubs retire his uniform No. 10.

"It will be my Hall of Fame," he said.

Santo reaffirmed that feeling a few moments before Sunday's ceremony at home plate in advance of the Cubs' final regular-season game.

"I meant that wholeheartedly," Santo said. "I'm not even going to worry about [the Hall of Fame vote] for the next two years" when he is eligible again.

Finally, after former teammates Randy Hundley and Glenn Beckert hoisted a flag bearing Santo's No. 10 up the left-field foul pole, Santo told 40,000 cheering fans: "This flag means more to me than the Hall of Fame. This is my Hall of Fame!"

Even the elements seemed to cooperate with Santo on his day. Just as he was being introduced, bright rays of sunlight broke through the cloud cover.

Realizing the significance of this phenomenon, Hall of Famer Ernie Banks smiled and pointed to the sun. The crowd broke into a wild cheer.

Santo was more than a Gold Glove third baseman who hit 342 home runs.

He played the game with such passion and enthusiasm that he forged bonds with fans of all ages and backgrounds.

This was evident Sunday by the people who approached him for handshakes or hugs.

They ranged from corporate big shots to Wrigley Field concession workers and ticket sellers.

Fans held signs expressing their feelings for Santo.

"Ron Santo, A Perfect 10" was the message on a huge banner on the screen behind left-field bleacherites.

"Wrigley Field Is Santo's Village" was painted on one bedsheet.

"Hall Of Fame Next, Ron" read another sign.

Another fan built his sign around the commercial for a credit-card company: "Hot Dog $3. Ticket To Game $36. 10-14-26 Priceless."

The last three numbers referred to the uniform

Santo's powerful swing hit 342 home runs over his 15-year career in the major leagues.

Santo is seen here with two other Cub legends Billy Williams (center) and Fergie Jenkins (right). The trio looks on as their former teammate Ernie Banks is honored with a statue outside Wrigley Field.

> ## This flag means more to me than the Hall of Fame. This is my Hall of Fame!
>
> —Santo when his No. 10 was retired by the Cubs

numbers of Santo, Banks and Billy Williams, the three Cubs whose numbers appear on the flag-poles at Wrigley Field.

Santo was severely disappointed early this year when he failed to poll enough votes to enter the Hall of Fame.

But Sunday, that rejection seemed the furthest thing from his mind.

When it came time for thanks, Santo remembered the Cubs organization, his former teammates, his broadcasting companions and the fans.

"The Cubs organization has completed my life, as far as I am concerned," said Santo, referring to the number retirement.

"I picked the Cubs because of Wrigley Field and Ernie Banks," Santo said. "I met Billy Williams when I was 18 years old in the minor leagues in San Antonio. We went on to play more games together than any two teammates, more than 2,000."

Speaking of the fans, Santo said, "This would not have been possible if it were not for all of you. You deserve a big hand. I wouldn't be here now if it weren't for you."

Santo then told the crowd what it most wanted to hear, drawing the loudest ovation of the ceremony when he said:

"And we're going to go all the way! I love you!" ■

Here Ron Santo is greeted by the handshakes of Billy Williams (center) and Ernie Banks (right) before the three honor the retirement of Fergie Jenkins' and Greg Maddux's No. 31 at Wrigley Field in 2009.

Teammates look on from the dugout at Wrigley Field as Ron Santo rounds third base on his 24th home run of the 1970 season.

By Dave van Dyck, *Tribune* reporter

# Best chance at Hall may come after death

## Changes to veterans voting could result in hollow victory

When his No. 10 was retired by the Cubs and hoisted above Wrigley Field, Ron Santo said it "means more to me than the Hall of Fame."

And he said it with a conviction that made you believe.

Whether he really, truly, down-deep meant it never will be known. His death Thursday left his last remaining baseball dream — election to the Hall during his lifetime — unfulfilled.

Nineteen times Santo was left waiting for the phone to ring on Hall of Fame election day, the last four votes coming from the Veterans Committee.

"I wanted it real bad, to be honest with you," Santo openly admitted after one of his letdowns.

He also said he didn't want to be elected after he died, but that could happen. In fact, it probably will because of changes in how former players are considered, by era instead of as one large group.

Santo falls into the "Golden Era" of players, executives, managers and umpires from 1947 to '72. That group — consisting of 10 names — will be voted on next December for possible induction in the summer of 2012 (this year's "Expansion Era" vote will be announced Monday).

With a 16-member committee of Hall of Fame players, executives and media, Santo would have to receive 12 votes.

He will be the favorite, having finished at the top of Veterans Committee voting in recent years. In 2007, he received 69.5 percent of the vote of Hall of Fame members. Last time, he received 60.9 percent.

Besides the persistent perception of not being good enough and the fact teammates Ernie Banks, Billy Williams and Fergie Jenkins have been voted in from a team that never won a title, his main competition will come from pitcher Jim Kaat, first baseman/manager Gil Hodges and outfielder Tony Oliva.

Like Santo, they failed for 15 years at making the Hall of Fame through the vote of Baseball Writers' Association of America members.

Maybe none of them will make it, but the rule change gives Santo his best chance — at what now would be a hollow victory. ■

Ronnie made his debut with the Cubs in the first game of a double header on June 26, 1960. Two days later this photo was snapped of the young third basemen.

Santo didn't reserve before and after games to sign autographs for fans. Here he is seen passing a freshly signed ball back to a fan during the game at the Cubs' spring training complex HoHoKam Park in Mesa, Arizona.

Told to Steve Rosenbloom

# OUT LOUD
# with Ron Santo

The Cubs' legend analyzes his days as a player, how he broke into broadcasting and his ongoing battle with diabetes with Our Guy

When I came up in 1960, we were averaging maybe 600,000 fans. In '69, we felt that was going to be our year. The fan base started to get larger and larger, and in '69 when we were in first place from the get-go, the "Bleacher Bums" — everything that was happening that year was unbelievable. You'd go on the road and you'd have the "Bleacher Bums" with you. You'd have fans there all the time. You knew the fans by their first name. And when we drew nearly 1.7 million fans for the first time ever, from that moment on, it's just gone straight up.

We were like rock stars. We always stayed in the clubhouse for two hours talking about the game, and we'd come out and we'd have 150 fans waiting. I had my shirt ripped off me once. You wonder what it would've been like if we'd have won.

Of course we should've won. I thought we were the best team that year in the National League. I felt the Orioles were probably the best team in baseball because of the pitching that they had. Yet, the Mets beat us and the Mets beat Baltimore. God lived in New York that year.

My dad left my sister and I when I was 6 years old. My mother and dad got a divorce. We were on the corner waiting for him to pick us up on weekends. He picked us up that first weekend and the second weekend, I never saw him again until I was 19. Then my stepfather came into my life when I was 12 and I call him Dad.

My mother had two jobs — waitress at a place in the afternoon, and then a drugstore. She'd come home about 10 o'clock and always with a smile on her face.

I think back to when I used to watch the "Game of the Week" on TV. The reason I tell you this is because that's when I became a Cubs fan. It was Wrigley Field, Ernie Banks, something about this ballpark and the Chicago Cubs.

To really tell the story, I ended up signing with the Cubs for the lowest amount. Everybody else was

Santo shares a laugh with former Cubs manager Dusty Baker before a game in 2008.

Santo is tagged out at home plate by San Francisco catcher Dave Rader in June 1972.

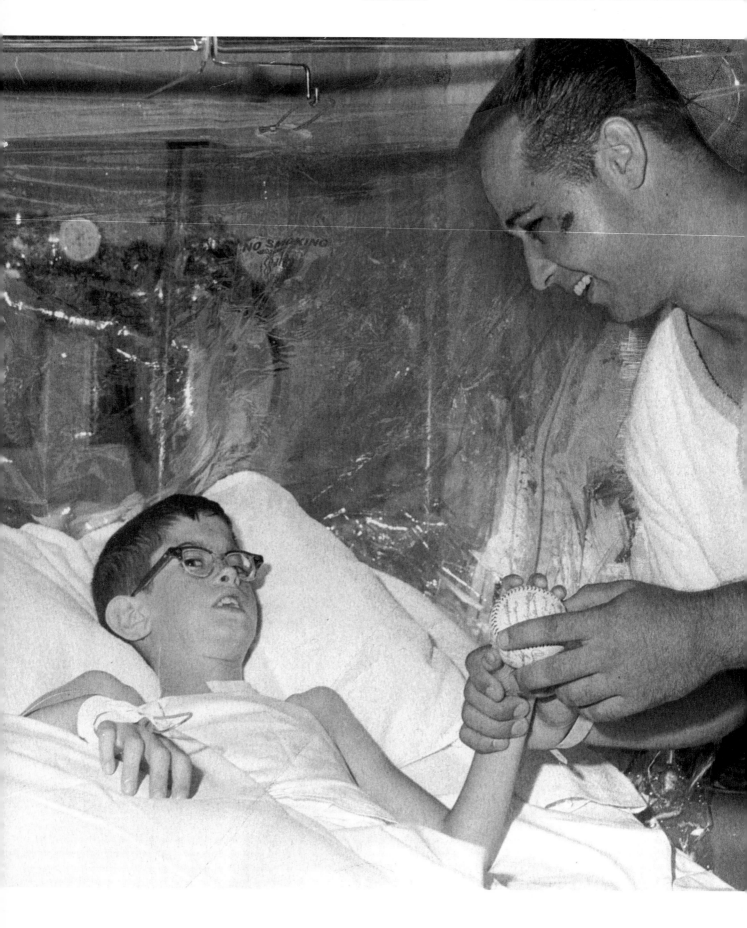

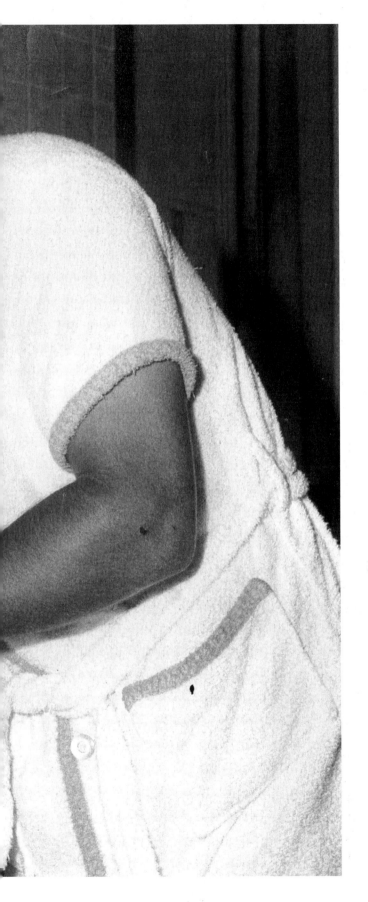

quite a bit higher, but I wanted to be a Cub.

My best baseball moment was when I came up on June 26, 1960. I was 20 years old and it was a doubleheader in Forbes Field in Pittsburgh. We were in a nine-game losing streak. Lou Boudreau was the manager. He put me in. I played both games. We won both games. First time up, I ended up getting a base hit up the middle. I ended up going 4-for-7 and driving in five runs.

At the audition to be Cubs radio analyst, I was so bad I can't tell you. I knew "5" was third base. I couldn't remember any other number. It was terrible. I had been out of the game for 17 years in business and done very well. So, we got done with the audition, and I went up to Bob Brenly — that's who I was auditioning against — and I said, "Bobby, congratulations. There's no way they're going to pick me. When you come to Chicago, we'll

(left) While recovering from being hit in the face by Mets' pitcher Jack Fisher in 1966, Santo cheers up a young patient with a handshake and a baseball. (above) Ron brings his own son Ron Jr. to the ballpark for a spring training game in Mesa, Arizona.

Santo flashes a grin at the camera before an August 2010 game against the Milwaukee Brewers at Wrigley Field.

Chicago Tribune Archive Photo

play golf." About a month later, they called and said they hired both of us.

I was six years with Thom Brennaman and then Pat Hughes came along. I just kept getting more comfortable with being myself. I make mistakes. It doesn't bother me. I laugh at myself.

This homer stuff is for the birds. I work for the Cubs, but I'm a Cub fan, so of course, I'm going to pull for the Cubs.

It's Type-1 juvenile diabetes/insulin-dependent my whole career. It's not that I couldn't let anybody know; it's that I didn't want to. I was in the big leagues when I was 20 with diabetes. If I didn't make it, I didn't want people to think that was the reason I didn't make it.

I made my first All-Star Game when I was 23, and that's when I announced it to my general manager and my teammates. I didn't announce it to the fans until my 10th year.

(left) Cubs TV broadcaster Len Casper sits between two Cub legends in Ron Santo and Billy Williams. (above) Ronnie shows Danny Murphy the bat that he hit his first major league home run with in 1960.

When I found out, I went to the library and read, and the first thing I read was that life expectancy for a Type-1 juvenile diabetic/insulin — dependent was 25 years. That's changed because of monies being raised since 1974 through JDRF and the federal government and now the NIH.

The best thing is going to the cure, and we're going to have that and I hope it's within my lifetime.

I had problems 10 years after I was out of the game with my eyes. I had laser, which they had perfected. I have over 5,000 burns in my right eye and over 4,000 in my left. I'm in remission. I had hardening of the arteries. In '99, I had quadruple bypass. In 2000, I was clean. In 2001, I lost my first leg. In 2002, I lost my second leg. I went through 23 operations. I went through a bout of cancer, but I got through that.

You know what? I feel I'm doing very, very well.

A few more wins — that's all I need. ▪

(left) Ron Santo performs a pregame interview for WGN Radio with Cubs manager Lou Piniella. (above) Santo slides safely into home plate for a victory against the Philadelphia Phillies in May of the 1973 season.

By Oscar Avila, *Tribune* reporter

# Santo fights daunting opponent: diabetes

Cubs legend admirers off the field, too, as a tireless supporter in the fight against diabetes. His charity work was exceptional.

Ron Santo enjoyed recounting a tense at-bat in the ninth inning with the bases loaded when his diabetes suddenly caused his blood sugar to plummet. That meant he was seeing not one, but three, fastballs coming at him.

"I hit that middle ball for a grand slam," he'd say.

The Cubs legend, however, did lose his share of battles with the disease, including when doctors had to amputate both his legs below the knee in the last decade of his life. That lengthy, grueling struggle meant that, of all his fans, few admired him as intensely as those living with diabetes or searching for a cure.

Santo was arguably the most prominent Chicagoan with the disease and helped raise an estimated $60 million for the Juvenile Diabetes Research Foundation through his annual Ron Santo Walk to Cure Diabetes that began in 1979.

"But it's impossible to gauge how much other support has come our way from people who were inspired from knowing Ron's story," said Patrick Reedy, executive director of the foundation's Illinois chapter.

"He wanted to make sure that all the challenges he faced in 50 years living with diabetes was not the same experience that a child diagnosed today would have," Reedy added.

Santo learned he had the disease during a routine physical after signing his first professional contract with the Cubs at age 18. Fearful that the team wouldn't keep him if it knew, Santo kept the diagnosis secret for years.

After going public, Santo poured himself into sharing his story. A 1972 Tribune article describes Santo participating in a summer camp at Lake Geneva, Wis., for children with diabetes. Santo signed autographs and told of living with the disease.

"We're no different than anyone else, except we take a shot in the morning," Santo told the children.

More recently, Santo's fight against the disease was a centerpiece of "This Old Cub," a documentary created by his son, Jeff. The film, in turn, inspired a

The 2010 season marked 50 years in Major League Baseball for Ron Santo. The Cubs honored the legend before the June 28 game against the Pittsburgh Pirates.

> **"Santo was arguably the most prominent Chicagoan with the disease and helped raise an estimated $60 million for the Juvenile Diabetes Research Foundation through his annual Ron Santo Walk to Cure Diabetes that began in 1979."**

former Elgin resident and longtime Santo fan to organize a 2,100-mile walk from Arizona to Chicago as a fundraiser.

As word of Santo's death circulated Friday, some fans on Twitter urged each other to donate $10 to the diabetes foundation in honor of Santo's uniform number. The Harry Caray's chain of restaurants said it would donate all proceeds from desserts sold through Sunday to the foundation, noting that the "desserts" category includes fruit and other items without sugar.

Santo's family also urged well-wishers to make donations, in lieu of flowers, to the foundation by visiting www.jdrfillinois.org and clicking on "Donate Now" or by calling 312-670-0313.

The news hit especially hard in the Rhode household in Burr Ridge, where the family knew Santo since shortly after daughter Cori was diagnosed with diabetes at 17 months. Now a senior at Lyons Township High School, she texted her father with word of Santo's death.

Ron Rhode said Santo's positive outlook had helped buoy the family. Typically meeting at one of his annual walks in the western suburbs, Santo would always ask about Cori's health. Then, he'd sit and patiently listen to fan after fan talk about their experiences, Rhode said.

"It's hard for Cori. There's ups and downs. Then you had Ron and he was up, up, up. There were no downs," Rhode said. "My daughter knew that when Ron talked about getting to a cure, he had the credibility that Dad didn't even have."

Having talked to Santo just two months ago, Rhode said the family feels as if they've lost a treasured uncle. Rhode grew up a White Sox fan in Oak Lawn but came to root for the Cubs after seeing Santo champion his daughter.

"It's a hard day today," Rhode said, "because we had someone in our corner and he's not there now." ∎

Aided by a cane to get to the mound, Ronnie needed no help throwing out this first pitch to start the 2003 spring training season.

By Ron Santo, as told to Paul Sullivan

# Here's why Wrigley Field is No. 1 to me

## Santo reflects on what makes baseball's shrine so special

I can only go back to when I signed with the Chicago Cubs to give you an idea of how I feel about this ballpark. I'd been watching it on TV in Seattle, where I was born and raised, and there was always something about Wrigley Field that intrigued me.

When I got here, two years after my senior year, I'm walking out of the corner clubhouse with Ernie Banks and there's nobody in the stands, and the feeling I had was unbelievable — walking with Ernie and walking on that grass. I felt like I was walking on air. There was an electricity and an atmosphere that I'd never experienced in my life. Any ballplayer that's ever played here can tell you about that great atmosphere, and anybody who's come here to watch a game feels the exact same way. This, to me, is a ballpark that helps the fans relate to the players because of its intimacy. They're right on top of you, and that's special. You look at a ballpark like Wrigley that holds 41,000, and it's packed every game, despite not having a team that's gone to a World Series in most of their lifetimes. People just love to come here, and it's a park you just love watching baseball in.

To me, it's the No. 1 park, and I think if you went and asked all the players who played here back in my day, they'd say the same thing. It's a hitters' ballpark, and everybody gets that feeling that anything can happen today. Everywhere you go, you see it. Cubs fans never lose their allegiance, or their love, for Wrigley Field.

Will Wrigley still be here in 50 or 60 years? I don't know that. I don't have an answer. Heck, I never thought I'd ever see Wrigley Field with lights, but they're here and they're great.

But I've got to believe that when you look at Wrigley, you're also talking about Wrigleyville. It's all about leaving the ballpark after the game and going to the bars and restaurants. It's one big happy family here, with nothing but parties. It's a wonderful place, and absolutely the best ballpark in baseball. ∎

Ron Santo, with his wife Vicky, acknowledges the crowd's applause at Wrigley Field.

Santo heads towards first base at Wrigley Field during the 1968 season. Santo hit 26 home runs for the Cubs that season.

By Steve Rosenbloom

# A mensch among boys

## Upon request, Santo sang at my son's bar mitzvah

Ron Santo would do anything for the Juvenile Diabetes Research Foundation, from leading a walk to hosting a golf outing, anything to raise money to find the cure

He'd even work a bar mitzvah.

In fact, he did.

My son's.

Back in July 2002, during the Cubs-White Sox series at new Comiskey, the Cubs were already mathematically eliminated — or something close.

"Ronnie," I said as just the two of us sat in the visitors' dugout, "it looks like you'll have your October free."

He snorted. I continued. I had a request.

I explained how my son, Brandon, would become a bar mitzvah in October, followed by a baseball-themed party on a Saturday afternoon. And how his mom, Karen, and I wanted to make a donation to JDRF in Santo's name if he would stop by to lead our guests in "Take Me Out to the Ball Game." Take five minutes. Only a 10-minute drive from his home. A small part of a Saturday afternoon. Whaddaya say?

Deal, Santo said.

As the Cubs' season ended with — are you sitting down? — another managerial change, I phoned John McDonough to ask him to wrangle Santo's memory and calendar.

That special day arrived. Brandon read from the Torah. Tears followed. Time for the party.

About two hours in, the kids were being organized into the hugging game (think musical chairs with hormonally charged 13-year-olds instead of furniture).

And then Santo walked in. Mazel tov.

The DJ told the kids to stop right where they were. I told everyone else to stand up and then brought Brandon and Santo on stage. I told our guests that we'd reached the seventh-inning stretch portion of our party, and I explained to the out-of-towners that this is how it's done on the North Side. We don't just sing the song. We have someone lead this tribal act. Conducting Brandon's would be Cubs legend Ron Santo.

Twelve-year-old Brandon Rosenbloom joins Ron Santo, his father, Steve, and mother, Karen, in singing "Take Me Out to the Ballgame" at Brandon's 2002 bar mitzvah.

> **Ron Santo would do anything for the Juvenile Diabetes Research Foundation, from leading a walk to hosting a golf outing, anything to raise money to find the cure. He'd even work a bar mitzvah."**

I gave Santo the mike. He immediately forgot Brandon's name. We certainly were getting the Full Santo. After a pause, I whispered, "A one, and a two..." and Santo got it going, full-throated on stage, ringing around the room. The Rosenbloom party made up for bad with loud.

I can't believe I still well up over this story. Two hundred people singing a song. So what, right?

But it was the one guy you'd want to lead this experience at a one-time event. There is no "We'll get 'em tomorrow" with a bar mitzvah. And Santo came through, bless him. And bless him now.

As he left the room, it was clear the kids could not have cared less. We stopped the hugging game for that?

The adults, though. Terry nearly pulled his wife's pitching arm out of socket, excitedly repeating, "That's Ron Santo, that's Ron Santo." I believe Barb was aware that was Ron Santo.

As Santo headed for the door, Vern caught him. "Ronnie," Vern said, his voice dripping of the exasperation that comes from being a Cubs fan all his life, "what are we going to do about the pitching?"

Some questions are forever.

Same goes for some Cubs. ◼

Ronnie was always full of energy, especially at the start of the season in Spring Training. Here he walks through the dugout in Phoenix, Arizona, after a few pregame interviews with players and coaches.

Ron Santo tags a sliding Lou Brock of the
St. Louis Cardinals as Brock tries to steal
third base during a game at Wrigley Field.

By Nina Metz, special to the *Tribune*

# At home, Santo leaves the color to the missus

## Santo reveals a life filled with love and simplicity

When he's not calling Cubs games on WGN Radio with play-by-play man Pat Hughes, "This Old Cub" Ron Santo (he's only 67) kicks back in his ranch-style three-bedroom home in the northern suburb of Bannockburn.

The house, which sits on an acre of land, is "traditional looking, but very comfortable," says the former third baseman and five-time Gold Glove winner. The decor is courtesy of wife Vicki. "She isn't in the design business, but she is really great when it comes to outfitting the home." The couple are owners of a dog (Joker) and a cat (Kitty), and once the off-season rolls around, they decamp for Arizona, where they have a four-bedroom ranch-style home that Santo says is decorated "Western-style. I'm a cowboy at heart. When I go out there, I got the boots and everything. We have three horses, by the way. I ride, and my wife shows quarter horses."

But back in Chicago, Santo doesn't have time for any of that. During the summer, it's strictly baseball.

**1. One thing on your nightstand:**
**My glucometer. I'm a diabetic, so I have my glucometer, my [hypodermic] needles. At night, I put a glass of orange juice in case of low blood sugar. I also have a clock and a lamp.**

**2. One thing on a wall in your living room:**
**We have a beautiful fireplace and wonderful built-in cabinets, so we don't really have any paintings on the wall. My wife is kind of an artist, a builder — she built a table out of a cactus plant. I got a 60-inch TV in there, and very comfortable leather seats.**

**3. One thing you have in your house from your childhood: I can't recall. No. Nothing.**

**4. Three condiments we would find in your refrigerator: Mayonnaise. Mustard. Would pickles be a condiment?**

After receiving the news that he had not been voted into the Baseball Hall of Fame by the Veterans Committee, Santo is consoled with a kiss from his wife Vicky in their Arizona home.

Ron sits with his daughter Linda Brown as he takes in the bad news of not being selected to the Baseball Hall of Fame. It was one of few accomplishments that eluded Ron, and probably one that upset him and fans most late in his life.

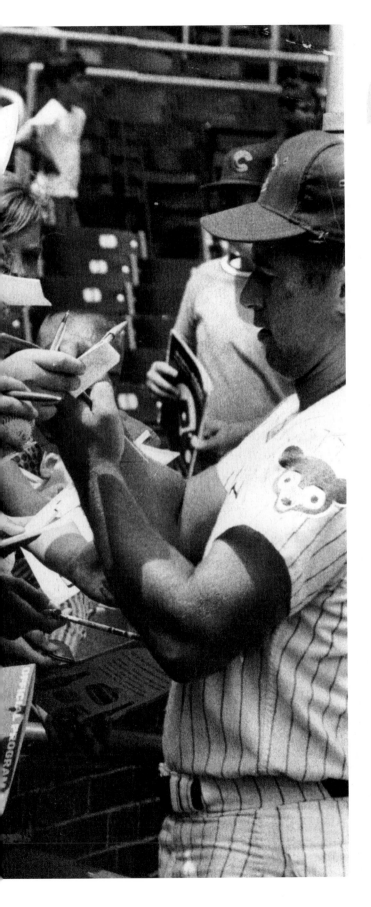

> **I'm a cowboy at heart. When I go out there, I got the boots and everything. We have three horses, by the way. I ride, and my wife shows quarter horses.**
> —Santo on his winter home in Arizona

5. Three things we would find in your medicine cabinet: **Shaving cream, mouthwash and deodorant.**

6. What reading material would we find in your bathroom? **A newspaper.**

7. Do your dirty dishes go in the sink or dishwasher? **Oh, dishwasher. Never never ever any dishes in the sink.**

8. Most high-tech gadget or appliance in your home? **I got 'em all. But don't ask me to tell you what they are. I can't think of any off the top of my head.**

9. Maker of your everyday dinnerware: **Oh, I have no idea.**

10. Maker of your fine china: **[Joking] Uh, it's called "Fine."**

11. If you had to save one "thing" from your home, what would it be? **There would be nothing. All I would be concerned about is getting out alive.** ∎

Even during his playing days Ron was willing to sign autographs for the fans. Here he is seen before a game in 1967 handing out as many signatures as he could.

Ron Santo interviews Dusty Baker for
a pregame broadcast for WGN Radio.

Phil Velasquez